AF255813

PERSPECTIVES

Perspectives

*Educational Poems on the
Humanities and Sciences*

Jim Hanson

RESOURCE *Publications* · Eugene, Oregon

PERSPECTIVES
Educational Poems on the Humanities and Sciences

Resource Publications
An Imprint of Wipf and Stock Publishers
199 W. 8th Ave., Suite 3
Eugene, OR 97401

www.wipfandstock.com

PAPERBACK ISBN: 978-1-6667-7761-1
HARDCOVER ISBN: 978-1-6667-7762-8
EBOOK ISBN: 978-1-6667-7763-5

05/17/23

Contents

Acknowledgments | vii
Introduction | ix

1. History

Empire Always | 3
Empire Relived | 6
Axial Age | 8
Scrapers | 10
Spider Schemes | 13
Passing | 14
Already Happened | 16
Time in a Museum | 18

2. Theology

Fatal Flutter | 23
God Killed | 24
God Dead | 25
God Chased | 27
God Embraced | 28
Becoming More | 30
Being God | 32
Voice of God | 34

3. Christianity

Walk with Jesus | 37
Who Was Jesus? | 39
God Guilty | 42

God Innocent | 44
Bible Babble | 45
Jesus Antichrist | 47
Eternal Now | 48

4. Buddhism

Walk with Buddha | 53
Sit with Buddha | 55
Walk with Nāgārjuna | 56
Dance with Shiva | 57
Mara | 59
Nothing Lost | 60
No Moon | 62

5. Taoism

Universe | 67
Emptiness | 69
Bent | 70
God | 72
Goo | 73
They Walk with Lao Tzu | 74
You Walk with Lao Tzu | 76

6. Philosophy

Derrida | 81
Nietzsche's Nihilism | 82
Plato's *Khōra* | 84

Leibniz's Question | 85
Sartre's Nothingness | 87
Heidegger's Nothingness | 89
Sartre and Heidegger | 91

7. **Language**

Words | 95
First Word | 97
No Word | 99
Moon Word | 100

8. **Science of Universe**

Chain of Being | 105
Out There | 108
Birth of the Universe | 110
Death of the Universe | 112
Betelgeuse | 114
Hubble's Eye | 115
Pioneer Ten | 117

9. **Science of Environment**

Chain of Living | 121
Once Upon an Epoch | 122
Too Late | 123
California Dreaming | 125
Good Times | 127

Water Waves | 128
Stromatolite | 129
Winged Migration | 130

10. **Other Science**

Endless Science | 133
Circling the Square | 134
Anthropic Principle | 136
Misanthropic Principle | 138
Light Thoughts | 140
Oneness | 142

11. **Poets**

Borges' Library | 147
A Bee after Emily D | 150
Eliot and Fear | 151
Eliot and Hope | 152
Gray's Elegy | 153
Jeffers' Prophecy | 155
Sylvia's Ironies | 157
Whitman's Song | 158
Whitman's Song Still
    Heard | 160
Yeats' Musings | 161

Acknowledgments

"Already Happened," *Nebo: A Literary Journal*, Fall 2018.

"Edges," *The Avenue: A Mid-Atlantic Literary Journal*, Issue VII, 2021, p. 93. https://theavenuejournal.squarespace.com.

"God Guilty," *Black Cat Literary Magazine*, Issue 2: Apocalypse, Autumn 2021, p. 14.

"Let Him Go," *International Journal of Fear Studies*, 2019, Vol. 2, University of Calgary Library PRISM (digital open-access). https://prism.ucalgary.ca/handle/1880/111140.

"Passing," *Harbinger Asylum* (by Transcendental Zero Press), Spring 2021. https://transcendentzeropress.org.

"Pioneer Ten," Illinois State Poetry Society, October 2021. http://illinoispoets.org/byauthor.htm#JimHanson.

"Plath's Ironies," *Otolith*, May 1, 2017. http://the-otolith.blogspot.com.au/2017/02/jim-hanson.html.

Introduction

Most poetry books need no introduction because they are collections with no specific theme or orientation. This book offers perspectives on the humanities and sciences. As indicated in the subtitle, it employs poetry to address the eleven perspectives of History, Theology, Christianity, Buddhism, Taoism, Philosophy, Language, Science of Universe, Science of Environment, Other Science, and Poets themselves. Its aim is to demonstrate how poetry can say something interesting and insightful about each perspective, with the ancillary aim of promoting interdisciplinary understanding in a liberal arts curriculum.

Poetry has the power to extend understanding through use of its analogies, metaphors, allusions, juxtapositions, and other figurative language, also through its minimalist provision of more meaning with less wordage. In this respect, it is unique, and needed to understand the generation of knowledge in other disciplines from an analogical as well as logical standpoint. It relates here to its sister disciplines in the humanities, including science at the calling of C.P. Snow to integrate the "two cultures." And it harks back to the first historians, religious believers, and philosophers who expressed themselves through poetry as Shelley's unacknowledged legislators of the world—a calling still needed today.

1

History

Empire Always

Herodotus sits on Mount Olympus
the gods now dead and legends gone
yet his works survive still this world as told
by Cicero the father of history

and from his view on high the centuries roll by
in time-lapse history always the same as
the sun above shines light and energy and as
storms of human conquest below cross the planet
drenching green land with red blood and
lighting horizons with the glory of gold.

So the great empires rise and fall over the
millennial ashes of fiery history
from Egyptian pharaohs to Microsoft wizards
their moment lauded universal and supreme
to end history—*temporis aeterni*

as they sail down rivers of civilization
cross over oceans of the globe
and rise into the skies of space,
reciting prophets of the axial age
and promising bright ages of timeless rule
as harbingers of art and industry
as moralists of justice and love and
as anointed saviors of life and death

yet promises needfully become lies
to cover the dark deeds of betrayal
by the conquerors of hearts and minds
who speak war as peace, ignorance as strength
in the recurring years of nineteen eighty-four

and their castles of sand wash
away in the ebb and flow of history
in average time of three hundred years
becoming eponyms of decline and fall
—Nineveh, Persepolis, Carthage,
Rome, Constantinople, Tenochtitlán,
Berlin, Tokyo, London, Moscow
with Beijing and Washington to follow

their rise and fall always the same game of
extorting taxes, exhorting order, exalting gods,
wielding weapons of stone, bronze and iron,
machines of war, bombs of uranium,
and ruling algorithms of silicone

and while history does not repeat
it rhymes no matter the times
as an ideology of warring opposites
monarchy/anarchy, democracy/autocracy
capitalism/socialism as us-versus-them
whatever the name always the same.

Now comes the greatest since Rome as the
exceptional shining republic of citizens
bestowed with liberty and justice for all
as states united—*e pluribus unum*

preceded by Caesars of Pax Romana and
now by presidents of industrial democracy

proclaiming free world leadership over autocracy
as west versus east and north over south

fulfilling Plato's prophecy of government
from aristocracy to democracy to tyranny,
fulfilling Toynbee's lifetime of civilization
from birth and growth to decline and death.

During the first rising of empire, when asked
why Greeks and Barbarians war against each other
Herodotus would say only, as a true Greek:
It ever was to be, always empire to seek.

Empire Relived

The old order fell
after European empires marched in
the blood of trenches soaked by millions
led by cousins George, Kaiser and Nicholas
into the twentieth century still shining from
the golden splendor of inbred aristocracies
imbibing in the conceit of Western civilization,

and the once proud and dutiful in the
internecine killing of their own
then staggered home with minds
shattered by PTSD and
by discontents of civilization
expressed in Victorian art:
expressionist painters soporific
songs and symphonies manic
Rudyard Kipling' s novels heroic
and Alfred Tennyson's poems prosaic.

The new disorder rose
as civilization disintegrated
witnessed by Spengler and Freud,
and day of divine right passed into the
stench of night from the bodies and empires
and slain by the swords of Mussolini and Hitler,

as the hoary ghost of empire ate its limbs of
liberté, égalité, fraternité
and marched once again to the
goose steps of duce, fuhrer, lebensraum
so that many more millions died
for the reliving of Roman grandeur
and purifying of a thousand year Reich.

The new order then rose with the dawn
of empires that fail to remember
and condemned to relive the history
of ageless desire for more empire
striving to last but destined to pass.

Axial Age

May we live in interesting times
is believed to be a Chinese curse
I hear as an American boast
about its century as ultimate history
of democracy over autocracy.

Every time is the most interesting
to the people who must live in it
and by their steadfast allegiances
including each generation of violence

against humanity of the twentieth
waging two hot world wars
with tens of millions dead
and one cold with lucky rolls
of thermonuclear dice

against nature of the twenty-first
waged by humans eight billion and more
spewing over the land and other life
to despoil earth, water, air and fire
to feed the fat in a new flat world.

So goes the Anthropocene Age
yet nobler centuries may be found:

my heart in the Nineteenth
of Beethoven, Nietzsche, Marx, Darwin
to feel the power to change by treason

my head in the Eighteenth
of Bach, Kant, Voltaire, Goethe
to feel the power to arrange by reason.

My spirit is in the beginning Axial Age
twenty-five centuries ago
when Yeats' ceremony of innocence began
with Socrates, Zoroaster, the Buddha and Lao Tzu
as the best having all conviction to reign
over the worst filled with passionate intensity:

Greeks debating thoughts along the Aegean Sea
Arabs reciting gathas on the Persian desert
Indians meditating under the Bodhi tree
Chinese eating analects of Tao in rice bowls

those who came, saw and transcended with care
the totems and taboos of pagan charm
Socrates, Zoroaster, the Buddha and Lao Tzu
who sought the higher and found salvation
who spoke truth and forged civilization.

O Jaspers
take me back to that Axial Age
when the world was only of the sage
where the future is the past
and the true may always last.

Scrapers

O mighty scrapers of the sky
riding high on earth rotations
to spite the forces of nature
gravity, water, fire, and air

rising by the dawn's early light
proudly hailed beyond twilight's gleaming,
powered by light over darkness of night
their steel unbending, cement unbroken
swaying to and fro courageously
unshakable, unbreakable, still there

shining as beacons of civilization
from mounds of earth in Cahokia
to scrapers of sky in Manhattan,
to be in the future seen and remembered
unbounded in space, uncounted in time
as a lasting triumph of human endeavor

mystifying as fountainheads of empires
for future generations to marvel about
the technology of how and ideology of why
workers by tens of thousands toiled to build
lifeless edifices of stone and steel,
by command for service and sacrifice
issued from authority regarded as god
and as mysterious as hieroglyphs

so viewed and revered as the
eternal statements of human spirit
over extinctions of the Phanerozoic Eon,
human civilization of the Anthropocene Age
reigning supreme—*Ecco Homo!*

Yet the ground beneath trembles
from restless tectonic plates
of moving continents and oceans,
bellowing fire and ash from deep
through the thin crust of earth and
shaking high mountains above

and fire and wind raze the surface above
as a beast without passion or purpose,
to grind under its feet constructions
dreamed and devised by humans and ants
as enterprising giants in the earth

set against the Anthropocene Age
following the five extinctions of nature,
trumpets sounding from the monuments
throughout history made by the imperial ages of
Egypt, Persepolis, Rome, Incas, Maya, Angkor Wat
and twenty-first century cities of
Dubai, New York, Kuala Lumpur, Shanghai

set against all scrapers that from giddy heights
dare to defy the limits of nature and laws of change,
their steel bending and concrete cracking while
teetering to and fro from ceaseless winds
then breaking and falling unable to stop
plunging ever faster down, down to the ground

where the broken remains of their age
lie silent to endure the humiliation of

crumbling apart one grain at a time,
dripping downward from the hourglass
watched helplessly by the Phoenix
also fated to the void of form as Solomon said
all go unto one place, from the dust and to the dust.

Spider Schemes

A spider
crawls up dark walls
spins its sticky web
kills its tangled prey
secures its silky world
hanging by a thread
of its own making

until swept away
by a broom made by

A nation
builds up high walls
defends its land
kills its terrorist foes
secures its boundaries
hanging by a treaty
of its own making

until swept away
by another nation.

So go schemes
of spiders and men

gang aft a-gley.

Passing

Seen through a looking glass
in light of each new day

people pass in silence
in an unbroken file

going onward always
dull eyes looking ahead

seeking home for rest and
solace within still walls

or looking out love for
a short day or long life

or reaching the rainbow
for gold had at the end,

but reasons matter not
just the passing matters

on tracks trodden by beasts
and tracked by hungry men

on trails ridden by
oxen and horses

on highways of hard oil
as machines belch and roll

passing through all eras
of the anthropocene

across land unmoved through
hills formed epochs ago

into the wind blowing
over trails of no end

under blue sky turned gray
when passing is to end

until morning lights the way
with another turn of earth

and passing begins again
as life moves along the way

seen the same just as before
moving through the looking glass.

Already Happened

It already happened
the moment you were born.

It's coming dead ahead through
the space of your life
the time of your life
a gamma ray burst
from light years away
speeding through space
as fast as light.

It's coming despite
the faith of your life
sublime in your life
not if but when
and without stop;
it waits not on you,
you must wait on it.

It's playing no game
no Pascal's wager
no luck of lotto
no luck at all.
The cards are Tarot
and the deck is stacked
with Thirteenth trump cards.

It's knocking at your door
locked from inside your room
lights turned out curtain drawn
hovering shadows and sounds
seen and heard in your mind.
None of this matters as
you lie sleepless in bed
seeking refuge from the night.

It's in here:
You reach forward to grasp
what is already gone
in a widening gyre
the brass ring never found
the kaleidoscopic colors askew
in the mayhem of inner darkness.

It's out there:
You arise and venture outside
in the night beyond neon lights
into shadows of a meadow
receding into the black sky
as tree leaves rustle in a quiet breeze
under the moon darkened by a white cloud.

You stop and stand motionless in the
unending dark to look up and see
what is coming that cannot be seen.

It already happened
the moment you were born.

Time in a Museum

Images in time on a museum wall:
Greek goddess posing nude and broken
her beauty unabashed and undaunted

Dutch merchant smiling with confidence
dressed in satin imported from the East

French peasant with scythe in a field
dwarfed by mountains and endless skies

Spanish harlot shaped in a cube
body pieces strewn in chaos.

As the bard of Ash Wednesday said
time is time and place only place

though dead in the past
they come alive in the present

told by a stoic look content
in a life-world different in time

a look that seems to know
they are being looked at

and living in their only place
to tell of their timeless story

of life lived only in the past
without a present or future

shown the same for me to know in
a moment of centuries ago.

I visit them as a voyeur ghost
coming backward from the present
and seeking to enter their past

imagining without knowing
what was then from what is now

walking among them unseen
and talking to them unheard

looking at their faces familiar
like my mother and father smiling

where all remain content in
the present of their time

and though I speak they do not hear
through the glass of another time

life gone and not be relived
remembered only in my mind,

and while visiting their bygone world
my spirit is touched by their presence

through images in a museum
where the present revives the past
sought by the memories of my mind.

2

Theology

Fatal Flutter

So it was to be:
God created
Mindful humanity
Universal law
World without flaw
Amen.

So it came to be:
Butterfly fluttered
Wind rippled
Earth shuttered
World crippled
So be it.

God Killed

We did not kill God, not The God.
We killed a god, a god invented by

>	J-Writer and Jews
>	Gospels and Christians
>	Qur'an and Muslims

>	Prophets forgotten in time
>	Legends and liturgies
>	Cave walls and computer clouds.

We did not kill the veritable God beyond our virtual god,
We could not ever kill the *Ein Sof* who was never

>	living and dying
>	evolving and emerging
>	coming and going

>	existing in space and time
>	speaking and choosing
>	saving and damning.

What is neither alive nor dead
must be left undone and unsaid.

God Dead

Per the death of God that came,
Poor Nietzsche usually gets the blame.
Proud Kant and Hegel deserved such fame,
Postmoderns prate and prance about the same:

    Airy vocabulary defames all exemplary,
    Le tout autre expands infinity to naught,
    Derridian *différance* deconstructs substance,
    Baudrillarian simulacra banalizes the word.

Nietzsche knew with certainty
Who killed God was not he
But we.
Yes we.

We first created God as a wispy other etched on cave walls and talismans,
then gave God a human shape and personality as a father, creator, ruler, judge,
to inspire prophets to idealize heaven and warriors to realize Armageddon,
then blamed and killed God as a theodic muddler of morality.

Where is the originary God undefiled by human history?
Perhaps lighting the fireworks of another Big Bang.
Perhaps as the absolute infinity of a unified field/world theory.
Perhaps beyond Chardin's Omega Point or an infinite algorithm.

Have we missed God in one place and failed to search another?
Perhaps God with Whitman stopped somewhere waiting for us.
Perhaps we sit with Godot and wait at the wrong place.
Perhaps we follow only Virgil and search the wrong realm.

Who knows the God not of our doing
that God beyond the God of our wanting
that God of nothing which is to say, no thing
but of pure being for our existence?

God Chased

God is the tail I chase in a circle
like a dog mistaking itself
for someone else.

As for God a circle does not matter
nor my mistaking someone else
coming back to myself.

As for me the circle will break
ending with no beginning
passing myself away.

I know only circles and squares
without an equation to
square the circle.

God knows the equation without fail
while I am the dog
chasing my tail.

God Embraced

God is your real idea as said

by Schopenhauer of the world

of polytheistic presence

with myriad forms and dimensions:

    word of holy texts such as
    Bible about God and Quran from God

    poetry of Rumi riding the wind
    or Milton resisting sin

    music of the spheres in perfect fifths
    and infinite octaves

    painting of Sistine Chapel
    and Mona Lisa smiling

    physics of the Higgs Boson as
    the God particle of mass fields

    biology of the abiogenesis of
    carbon hydrogen nitrogen oxygen phosphorus

mathematics of constants
immutable and universal

light of energy and yang,
mass of matter and yin

essence of language,
transcendence of spirit.

You are God's idea as revealed

in the Garden of Eden, also the Stromatolite

in all of its apotheotic presence

as another vain idea by you of God.

Becoming More

You are more than

energy scattered across formless fields
as timeless flickering in string theory

particles speeding from and to
positions random and unknown
in the uncertainty principle

elements of CHNOPS
lumped together as life
in the beginning with microbes

animals fighting over territory
to pursue survival of the fittest

homo sapiens thriving in society
to pursue collective power as a

soldier of national quest
believer of religious sect
carrier of economic portage
captive of societal bondage.

You are more like

Mandelbrot's fractal of
forms of mass to matter
reflecting divine design.

Einstein's dice of certainty
always rolling up seven
to conform with cosmic laws

da Vinci's Vitruvian man
the perfect universal form
wherein circles and squares are one

God's chosen species of the universe
with language-based intelligence knowing
the law and nature of all things and forms.

Are you still more like

a being above being
unfettered by place and time
transcending your existence

a spirit out of body and mind
breaking through finite boundaries
free to be all possibilities

an image of god
knowing good and evil?

Being God

You can be God
all you can be and infinitely more
outside the contours of the universe

which is your understanding of
all that can be possible
outside boundaries of space and time.

God can be you
all God can be and infinitesimally less
than the quantum field of the Higgs particle

which is your potential as another
sentient being blessed and blessing others
existent as either mortal or immortal

understood by your cosmic consciousness
to reach beyond real of omnipresence
and to know beyond truth of omniscience.

Cataphatic penetrates apophatic as
the Godhead shines through divisions of trinity
illuminating the world with the divine

inspiring human creature creations of
Shakespearean drama and Beethoven symphony
Thomastic thought and Einstein relativity

transforming the finite of immanence
into the infinite of transcendence
and potentiality into possibility

merging the immortal being of God
with the mortal existence of yourself
so God may be in you and you in God.

Voice of God

The wind is the voice of God
unheard and always moving
unknown from where or when
yet bringing calmness
to your restless soul.

Listen carefully
and you will hear
this cosmic wind faraway
blowing in through space and time
from beyond the universe
and into the channels of your mind.

Do you hear it?

Try easier.

3

Christianity

Walk with Jesus

You want to walk with Jesus
down the Mount of Olives road
laden with clothing by those

who love you as their father
who loves them in return

but be careful who you walk with.

Your destination is Jerusalem
yet you tremble at its danger

darkened by imperial power of Rome
deprecated by Pharisees jealousy
desecrated by greed within the Temple.

Your destiny is Calvary
as the hill of crucifixion

where you want to be remembered
there with him to forgive them
who know not what they do.

You want to walk in his footsteps
into the history of his name as

the messiah of love and peace
although the road is dangerous

the chosen son of the holy Father
although the body is sown with sin

the anointed saint whose soul is perfect
although in the end feeling forsaken.

No, you do not walk in his footsteps
to find the way

but you can fall upon your knees
to seek and pray.

Who Was Jesus?

Jesus twelve-year-old prodigy
missing for three days in Jerusalem
found lecturing teachers in the temple
until taken home to live in obedience

and nothing more said
by Luke or other apostles
nor read in the gospels
or church catechisms.

Fade-out.
Fade-in, eighteen years later.

Jesus twenty-nine-year-old stranger
appears by the Jordan River
baptized by John
proclaimed as the messiah
at the opening of the heavens

and those who knew the boy
questioned the man who spoke
of God in opaque parables
—Where did he go? What did he do?

A local, uneducated carpenter
whose knowledge came straight from God
so the imperial churches and kings said

through Nicene creeds and centuries of
purging and purifying influences deemed pagan
including Jewish.

Thus began the greatest stories ever told
too great for one bible or church or
by apocryphal tales of James, Thomas
or by others pagan and heretical
all making Jesus many things: son of God
the Christ, Jew, Gnostic, Prophet, Messiah

and an Essene who in his lost years
found Judea's ascetic monastics
to study and write the Dead Sea scrolls
long lost in the Qumran caves
a day's walk from Jerusalem

among the Essenes who came from Alexandria
one hundred-fifty years earlier
and who emerged there after Buddhists came
as emissaries of the Indian king Ashoka
known as the Therapeutae philosophers
who stayed and established temples

and as an Essene the young Jesus learned
the wisdom of the ages—Jewish, Greek, Egyptian
Zoroastrian of Persia and Buddhist of India—
also by traveling to Egypt, Asia Minor and maybe Kashmir
to be known as Issa across the East
from Mesopotamia to China.

The greatest stories were imported sequels
from the legend five hundred years before Jesus
depicting the life and teaching of the Buddha
who predicted a savior in five hundred years
and became a model for the legend of Jesus:

conceived by a god
divine birth at midnight
birth presided by a star
manifested prodigious childhood
consecrated in a holy river (Ganges)
sought isolation in early years
defeated the devil (Mara)
predicted and heralded as a savior
began ministry thirty years old
performed miracles and walked on water
opposed by religious elite (Brahmin)
recruited twelve main disciples
held incantations and beatitudes
cured illness and blindness
comforted the poor
professed love, peace and golden rule
addressed sin and suffering
taught mostly by parables
recognized in book with seven seals
predicted second coming.

Two world religions launched
from a base of hallowed trinities:
Buddha/Sangha/Dharma, Father/Son/Holy Ghost

different at their present but similar in the past
history repeating not the time but still with rhyme
to what was then and once again to begin

Jesus' spiritual journey thereupon consummated
as the Jewish Messiah presaged by the Buddhist Maitreya
to live in permanent history and perennial philosophy.

God Guilty

By Cosmic News Network

At his trial in the Milky Way District God was found
guilty of manslaughter after his chosen species
devastated the environment and caused
life extinction across the planet of Earth.

Prosecutors argued that the Garden of Eden was
the primal crime scene where God failed to vet Adam and Eve
then exiled them to earth to introduce sin and to
pollute and despoil its life-sustaining environment.

Prosecutors stressed willful negligence because
God failed to use his omniscience to detect flaws
of character exposed at the Tree of Knowledge and
to use his omnipotence to annul the result.

Prosecutors claimed God violated cosmic law
and intervened to assist the homo sapiens species
without due diligence and with reckless disregard
for the right of ascension by alternative species.

Defenders argued manslaughter was unavoidable
due to flaws in the universe, biological laws
allowing human ascendance based on competition
and physical laws that included entropy and death.

Defenders also argued other species were not
fit alternatives but did not refute arguments
that ants and toads were more cooperative and peaceful
and grasshoppers who were also vegetarian.

God was sentenced to be exiled from the Universe and
his whereabouts in other universes remains unknown.

Back on Earth healing began as amoebic life in the
oceans scheduled to come on land in ten million years.

God Innocent

Theists Deists Atheists agreed
to rule God innocent
although once thought guilty to be
at the scene of crimes by Humanity
and to mastermind crimes of evil.

Evidence pointed to God's complicity
by creating Humanity and
providing means and opportunity
to kill life on Earth through
illegal use of technology and science.

However:

Theists said
God was here and did his best
but Humanity failed the test
at the Garden of Eden.

Deists said
God there was never here
and stayed away in fear
of Human crimes on Earth.

Atheists said
God was never here or there.

Bible Babble

Oh death where is thy sting?
Though I walk through the
valley of the shadow of death
I fear no evil.
    —15:55–58 Cor

So I'm walking . . .

down here . . .

still farther . . .

more shadows . . .

getting dark . . .

path gone . . .

so what . . .

spooky folktale . . .

stupid talk . . .

stupid walk . . .

seen enough . . .

coming back up . . .

just step over this

a
    b
        y
            s
                s
                    . . . .

Jesus Antichrist

Most people think the Trinity odd:
Does Jesus still live as Spirit and God?
Jesus was a Jew but Jews are not sure;
on Jesus as Spirit and God they demur.

According to John, Christ lived on
canonized as God's only son
who set oceans and continents afire
salvation wrought by soldiers of empire.

Jesus became Christ and Christ Christendom:
good news for believers of Christ to come
but not so heard by followers like me
who love only Jesus of Galilee.

Eternal Now

You pray with Paul Tillich
in the eternal now:

birth comes from the egg for
you and the universe

time and motion stop with
each breath everlasting

day shines into night
making shadows glow

truth appears through
a glass brightly

music plays beyond the score
with notes soaring into space

love whispers through the air
in voices of pure sound

heart beats march forward
to infinity

life spreads across all
four corners of earth

dreams show the way
to quests of life

leaves age on grass for
for poets to wonder.

His God beyond god
answers your prayer

yet eternity may be
just one moment of the now.

4

Buddhism

Walk with Buddha

Walk with the Buddha into Nirvana
where world suffering is blown out
casting away the winds of karma and
quelling the desire of life and fear of death.

Walk into the dwelling of the three refuges:
Buddha's fourth jhana of pure equanimity
Dharma's release from life and death of samsara
Sangha's meditative silence and oneness.

Walk the path of no boundaries
covered by leaves of change on formless grass
beneath trees of seeds blown into space
marked by pure light empty of shadows.

Walk upon the freely moving wind
rising feet never touching defiled ground
levitating into endless space and time
joining ten thousand things in ten directions.

Walk through the emptiness of form
with no adjacent space of here and there
or sequential time of now and then
and with body and mind left behind.

Don't walk, no steps really needed
sit and abide in destinations
already here in your motionless mind
through which walking comes and goes.

Sit with Buddha

Mara
swoops down
from the sixth heaven
with demons of dread
fire and fury
with daughters of desire
samsara defiled.

Buddha
sits unmoved
at the bodhi tree
smiling in silence
fourth jhana of equanimity
peace and purity
nirvana undefiled.

Done
for all buddhas
facing dread and desire
in the middle way
between life and death
not moving to either side
filling a world to abide.

Walk with Nāgārjuna

Walk the middle of the path between the
lines of affirmation and negation

affirming lines closing the path to emptiness and freedom
negating lines deleting the path to form and structure.

The path is true and made by nature.
The lines are false and marked by humans.

Walk the path and you'll be fine
straight through space and bent through time

hand-in-hand with Nāgārjuna
from karma into nirvana.

Dance with Shiva

Dance with Shiva to celebrate
the cosmos—dark cold empty
to be humanized with eternal energy
over timeless creation and destruction
with preservation, illusion and emancipation

perpetual creation and destruction
known in the Jātakas as the Cyclic Uproar
occurring every one hundred thousand years
across the earth and up the Brahma heavens.

Dance as the single being of Shiva
at the center of the universe
its aureole circling around you

and transforming dark matter
of particles and galaxies
into flames of light and heat from the
fusion and fission of adorning suns.

You rule the cosmos and
consciousness of Brahman
eternal and constant beyond
Eddington's arrow of time and
edges of the known universe
where nothing is known yet seen
only with Shiva's third eye

and you keep dancing lest
the fire of the aureole dissolves
and energy becomes the entropy
of the cosmos gone dark and lifeless.

If too apotheotic for you
then dance with Native ghosts to rise
against Federal reservations
or dance with Leonard Cohen
to the end of love to be renewed
or dance to destroy Zabriskie Point
to create the Age of Aquarius.

What matters is the energy of dance
flashing throughout the cosmic night
to throbbing cycles of death and life
of human lifetimes and ages
of other worlds in space and time
and universes beyond space and time

and your celebration of Shiva
great holder of nature's forces
the creator of destruction
and destroyer of creation.

Mara

Mara
swoops down
from the sixth heaven
with demons of dread
fire and fury
with daughters of desire
samsara defiled.

Buddha
sits unmoved
at the bodhi tree
smiling in silence
fourth jhana of equanimity
peace and purity
nirvana undefiled.

Done
for all buddhas
facing dread and desire
in the middle way
between life and death
not moving to either side
filling a world to abide.

Nothing Lost

You hold onto life but
you come from nothing.
What have you to lose?

You put off death but
you go to nothing.
What have you to gain?

High from a tree with teeth clinched to a branch
you are asked what to do to save your life
you want to recite the Lord's Prayer for redemption.
How do you say?

Climbing a one hundred-foot pole
you finally arrive at the top.
How do you advance?

You make a cart with twenty spokes
and take away its box and axel.
What do you have?

You ask what is Buddha
and you are told shit on a stick.
What do you learn?

You are told the dharma
is not mind, Buddha, or beings.
What do you think it is?

Show your face before you were born.
Nothing pictured nothing feigned.
Nothing ventured nothing gained.

Show your face after you died.
Do it now while still alive.
Nothing lost
     Nothing
        Not
           No
              n
               ∞

No Moon

Nothing is itself except if known
and if known is no longer itself:

no man as known in the moon
no trace as seen of a face

no moon except dirt and rock
no moon the same as the name

no moon in the image of an eye
no moon near in a pond seen so clear

no heavenly body if
drawn to earth by gravity.

Moon is empty because it exists
and exists because it is empty

of sights seeing what it is not
and words naming what it is not

not about the man it is not
and all about itself it is

so looking for the dark side
is how to find the bright side.

The moon is seen and known
just as the Buddha said

no perception or conception
no sight or word inside your head.

5

Taoism

Universe

Lao Tzu sits on the
green, walking mountain
musing about the great Tao
from which everything flows
to which everything returns
like water flowing down to earth
and returning to heaven above.

This Tao so fickle and uncaring,
treating ten thousand under heaven
as straw-dogs to be made
then burned and thrown in the street
inhumanely with no regard,
not even for God as a being
it precedes and begets.

This Tao child of parents unknown,
seeming ancestor of ten thousand beings
rising and falling from its being
and its being from nonbeing
(baffling even to Heidegger)
from emptiness beyond the edge
of unknown space and advent of time
bursting into existence as a
big bang to create a universe
from disentangled particles broiling in soup
then alphabetic elements entangled

to form far-flung stars and galaxies
expanding beyond known existence
out to unknown emptiness.

This Tao beyond naming,
known only to mere beings
that it is that it is
whether from moving mountain
burning bush or lotus flower
pouring yet inexhaustible
emerging yet unfathomable
empty yet boundless.

So say sages as beings sitting
on mountains between earth and heaven
seeking to know being unknown
beyond bounds of their existence.

Emptiness

Said old Lao Tzu to the Chang/Zen sages
who followed: As good to be good requires bad,
so existence to be existence requires emptiness

and not just for the self easily dismissed,
but for the space of here requiring there
and for the time of now requiring then

for how could you be here if not for there
and how could you be now if not for then?
Existence, space, time, everything empty!

Tis bad news for the popular here-now
proclaimed by professors of positivity
who dismiss past memory and future plans

who claim instant reality
and deny all that is empty
in a half-filled glass of water.

But despair not—empty is an opening
to see beyond existence named and counted
in distance of space and duration of time

to leave measures of existence
and extend in all dimensions
into infinity of Tao.

Bent

If to go straight for broke, then broke
you will be like Humpty Dumpty
in his fall, and no omelet is yet made
from an egg or by men,
only scattered pieces that super glue
cannot put back together again.

Tis a story told not just for the young
but for the old prone to pondering
ancient conundrums, as said by Taoists:
Bent preserves the whole,
so the broke falls into a hole
affirmation turned to negation.

Lines of nature everywhere bend
like palm trees in a hurricane,
not straight and broken or gone to
extend into infinite nothing
but curved and kept to return
to the top of the circle,
wont to moving around from
here going down and there going up,
bent preserving the whole.

Lines of matter bend from
then going out and now back
to form planets and stars

always round and never square,
and light moving through space-time
yielding to gravity of mass as
no mere refraction of perception,
instead universal workings of
special and general relativity,
bent preserving the whole.

Lao Tzu knew centuries ago
that eggs falling straight would break
but matter and light could bend,
that Einstein is a Taoist.

God

We know not its name
just its alias—God.

The name that is named
is not the everlasting name.

The God that is named
is not the everlasting God.

Tis a whirling emptiness
yet is inexhaustible.

Tis beyond ten thousand things
unceasing and fathomless.

Tis a hidden mystery
manifest without desire.

Tis a consequent of
Tao the antecedent.

We know its name as the
God of nameless Tao.

Goo

Tao is the grinding churn
where we come and return.

We cheer the coming
but fear the return.

Yet life was no fuss
not for old Lao Tzu.

Tao still sticks to us
as life's primal goo.

They Walk with Lao Tzu

They walk with Lao Tzu
unknowingly, dangerously
beyond distance of space
and duration of time

into the unknown being of Tao
nameless, formless, silent, empty
unfathomable yet ever present
inexhaustible yet ever pouring.

Most who sought and thought to know the world
misunderstood the futility
of their ceaseless naming and aiming
for solutions final and finite:

Lucretius who had entangled atoms
falling disentangled

Aristotle who told of the mover
moving all things but unmoved itself

Schopenhauer who limited sufficient reason
by the unknown thing-in-itself

Heidegger who told of the infinite being
of all finite beings

Heisenberg who found the principle
of uncertainty in particles

Eliot who saw ending as beginning
and beginning as ending

Yeats who foretold the second coming of
things falling apart and center not holding.

Tillich who sought the unknown god
beyond the known god.

Most walking with Lao Tzu are
ten thousand straw dogs bound by earth
living inhumanely, clinging vainly
to the names and forms ignored by Tao.

You Walk with Lao Tzu

Walk with Lao Tzu not there
like the Tao not here
but everywhere.

You know without knowing
Tao is always unknown
by knowledge not lasting.

You name without naming
Tao is always unnamed
by language not lasting.

When severed from Tao
you walk with the straw dogs
among ten thousand things.

When united with Tao
you walk into the origin
of heaven and earth.

Tao is like wood
when uncarved left for good
but when carved used for bad.

Tao is the cosmic egg
from which all things emerge
to which all things return.

Tao is the great sponge
dripping out the water of life
absorbing the decay of death.

Tao is the pure calm
before the storm of action
when nature is inhumane.

Tao is what it is
not for you to have
because it has you.

Walk with old Lao Tzu
while knowing and trusting
Tao is life's primal goo.

6

Philosophy

Derrida

As a seeker of postmodern truth
I deconstruct my poem of groundless text
cutting up and blacking out suspect words,

thinking semantics and metaphysics are dead
thinking poets since Bill Burroughs had it right:
seeing is believing, trust nothing beyond sight.

Yet maybe wrong are these deniers
of words of truth and truth of words
and wearied of philosophical skeptics,

I fall asleep and dream of Dorothy
walking through green forest and black witches
on the winding yellow road to escape,

ending before a curtain and voice
to see only a small, white-haired man
named Derrida to speak a frightful truth:

Nothing exists beyond the text of our making.

Nietzsche's Nihilism

The horse was old and stubborn
stumbling with withered body
but deliveries must be made and
as the merchant took whip in hand
a man came running forward
to grasp the neck of the horse
and plead in broken Italian—Stop!
then collapsed on the stone pavement
and wept in indistinct German

that gray winter day in the street
of Turin in eighteen eighty-nine
when Friedrich Nietzsche lost his mind
—paralytic dementia the doctors said
of Europe's great philosopher
who would shake European thought
by the great noontide march of
Übermensch whose will to power
promised the humanist nihilism of the
last decadent man and Christian-conceived God

that winter day when Nietzsche was
broken by his own will to power
—Aryan man of destiny, the Nazis said
prophetically about their own destiny—
and in his remaining twelve years
never again uttered a word of sense

although he played the piano
that then too fell away to
sounds heard only from madness,
thus wept Zarathustra.

Plato's *Khōra*

Long before modern nihilism
Plato pondered upon *khōra*,
the receptacle of formlessness
as the existential foundation
of all things shown and known.

Nonsense, the men of Athens said
for we stand firmly on the ground,
to which Socrates replied:
If no space is in and about the ground
how could you or me be found?

(And in China at this same Axial Age
Lao Tzu told skeptical men the same:
The origin of all things had no name
only the nameless eternal Tao
from which nothing could be shown or known.)

Leibniz's Question

Leibniz's famous question:
Why is there not nothing?
as if he wanted
nothing or
more of it

yet nothing is
already more
much much more
than something
or anything
in an atom
or galaxy.

A better question:
Why is there not something
or at least
more of it
and less
of nothing?

because something is
already less
than nothing
or anything
whether in physics
or poetry.

And Leibniz
surely knows
less must be
more than more
and more is
less than less.

Sartre's Nothingness

Jean-Paul Sartre his human being at risk
scribbled on a pad inside Café de Flore
hiding in a dark corner during winter cold
ruminating about being and nothingness
as Nazi troops marched down Rue Saint Benoît.

Philosopher of being
professed on being-in the world's totality
and its landscape of infinite objects
illuminated from particles to galaxies
and pregiven to consciousness of what is.

Philosopher of nothingness
professed on being-for the world's nihilation
and its landscape of finite objects
to be burned by the fire of desire
by the consciousness of what is not.

Hero of freedom
pondered on how to escape from others
and nihilate things as given objects and
yet to be condemned to the consciousness
of existing in the angst of nothingness.

Victim of oppression
condemned to a room in perpetual light
to endure the hell of being with people

who before the open door take no exit
toward responsibility of choosing freedom.

He echoed ancient Greek tragedy of
Dionysian passion over Apollonian rationality
the mind ravaged by the forces of desire and will
as projects of madness done by Oedipus and Electra
and savaged by the nihilative forces of willful gods:
floods of water and quakes of earth by Poseidon
disasters of wind by Aeolus and fire by Hephaestus.

He echoed other legends of
yin the female earth of passive plenitude violated
by yang the father fire of active purging
and Vishnu creator of form negated
by Shiva the destroyer of form
and Yahweh creator of humankind canceled
heaven by exiling Adam and eve from Eden.

Jean-Paul Sartre now sits in the Round Robin Bar as
deniers march down Pennsylvania Avenue
and types his blog to ruminate about the
being of the environment nihilated by
desire and will of industrial development
and about the oppression of freedom
and repression of existence
in a world with no exit.

Heidegger's Nothingness

Martin Heidegger Black Forest philosopher
dwelled in the forbidding forest of Ardennes

remaining being-there (da-sein) throughout his life
yet shaking the world of philosophy

his da-sein haunted by being-toward-death of
Germany in the Great War and destined for more.

He looks for a path through trees and brush
of overgrown rhetoric and metaphysics

to an opening of understanding where
the light of Being shines on all beings

to be seen unconcealed and revealed
as self falls away into Nothingness:

>   no I of Descartes
>   no person of Shakespeare
>   no self of Freud or Whitman
>   no soul of Plato or Augustine

and as crusted concepts crumble and
old dispositions are abandoned:

not idealized by Plato's dialogues
not bargained as done by Goethe's Faust
not played in chess as Bergman's Seventh Seal
not calculated as per Pascal's fallback wager.

He will speak in ontological maxims
about the Being and Nothingness of beings:

    Nothingness negating beings
    Being predating beings
    Being containing Nothingness
    Nothingness constraining Being.

and replace old metaphysics
with an older ontology

    following the truth of Aristotle
    and romanticism of Hölderlin
    back to the forest clearing as home
    before the century of world wars

    when Being was kept pure by
    the innocence of Nothingness.

Sartre and Heidegger

Sartre and Heidegger came to be
great sons of France and Germany

philosophers of being
and nothingness of dread

famous around the world
their many books all read

met in nineteen fifty-three
to advance ontology

about how being turns to nothing
which certainly would have been something,

instead they argued throughout the day
with nothing about nothing to say

thereby left ontology
as a mere tautology

so their world remained the same
with themselves only to blame.

7

Language

Words

Words, words—too many
few if any needed, fewer still heeded
for the real world disclosed by
Heidegger's there-being of dasein
always out there and in here as well

real world remade by myriad dualisms
and divided as mind or matter, yes or no
by using words of finitude to
name the world of infinitude

no need for Descartes's thought
no heed to Bergson's nought.

Words, words—too remote
each pointing at each thing started by
monkeys squawking high in trees,
spitting down each letter whether
of d-o-g or g-o-d
when all about bananas

each joining only other words
of dictionaries in thin air
and floating over earthly things,
notwithstanding consequences of
wrong names and low probabilities

each laying claim to Kantian certainties
remembering only A=A and not B.

Words, words—how many left
after modern deconstruction of
nouns of subjects and objects condemned by Heidegger
adjectives and adverbs slain by Gertrude Stein
auxiliary verbs purged by Wittgenstein
and passive verbs struck by William Strunk

and never trusted by mystics to name God
or Taoists to name a world everlasting.

Even loquacious positivists must
obey what Wittgenstein would say
that what not spoken demands silence
no reliance upon word or its world
only nothingness of silence

yet to be alive happenings do arrive
no matter what the word as subject-object
adjectives to describe or bad verbs to imbibe,
there is the verb intransitive to objects
therefore no need for subjects

saying only saying, praying only praying
none of other needed, few if any heeded.

Words, words—too few
to disclose infinite being,
break through the unnamed silence
and to make up the happening
known only by Tao and God

otherwise unknown but for
the world known through human words.

First Word

The word of the journey was heard:

about Achilles and Odysseus
seeking fame and dominion

by proud poets going back to Homer
touting heroes of a thousand faces

in telling each journey as a story
of happy news and great man history

with inspiring ideology
and enduring immortality.

But the first word was blurred:

in the epic of history's first hero
Gilgamesh who journeyed for fame in vain

who doomed Endiku to early mortality
and failed to obtain his own immortality

who returned to Uruk to seek forgiving
and whiled away his last time of living

who peeled an onion to find no less
the center to be mere nothingness.

The message of the first word becomes slurred
by a hero lauded for wealth and rule

whose beginning travels through history
turned out to be illusory and cruel.

No Word

In the beginning was The Word

> said by God on high to fill
> the void and light the darkness

> heard by Adam in Eden
> to learn of good and evil.

What if

> the word were not heard
> let-there-be not said

> the word forever heard
> to make the world absurd

> the word not intelligible
> because no Rebus Principle

> the word not in real conversation
> only self-centered motivation

> the word and world not quite the same
> order and meaning never quite came

> the word and world in the Anthropocede
> to the Cambrian Period would recede.

What if the above were true, at least partly?

Moon Word

Nothing is itself except if known
and if known is no longer itself:

no man as known in the moon
no trace as seen of a face

no moon except dirt and rock
no moon the same as the name

no moon in the image of an eye
no moon near in a pond seen so clear

no heavenly body if
drawn to earth by gravity.

Moon is empty because it exists
and exists because it is empty

of sights seeing what it is not
and words naming what it is not

not about the man it is not
and all about itself it is

so looking for the dark side
is how to find the bright side.

The moon is seen and known
just as the Buddha said

no perception or conception
no sight or word inside your head.

8

Science of Universe

Chain of Being

The universe is always the same
after you go and before you came.

The first law of thermodynamics
has the conservation of matter and

leptons streaking safely in space as
indestructible information even

from black holes. The second law of
thermodynamics has matter deform

as energy and energy reform
as air, water and earth of matter.

The theory of abiogenesis
has the molecules of oxygen,

hydrogen, nitrogen and phosphorus
evolve as bacteria, then up to

multiple-celled Eukaryotes, to central
nervous systems with sensory organs,

to limbic and mammalian brains, and to
symbol-making minds, all by the laws of

infinite emergence and complexity
extending the evolution of life itself

from the actuality of phylogenesis
to the potentiality of ontogenesis.

The chain bends into a circle back to
ashes of matter and energy as

alternating complexity of Lucretian
atoms entangled and disentangled

and back to the life and death of
organisms and universes

all reenactments of Nietzsche's
doctrine of eternal return.

The chain sparkles like Indra's net
with each jewel a portal to stars

glistening to show the way
to the presence of the Tao

perhaps to Plato's khōra
or Tillich's God beyond gods

all pointing beyond human being
to primal being not seen and known

through existence of having and doing
past the edge of space and the end of time.

The links of the chain are unbreakable
and its lengths are unfathomable, and

you want to ride the train down the chain to
enter the mysteries of primal being

from whence all things come and thence they go
ever there but never yours to hold.

Out There

They are out there
in the black of space trillions of miles away
there on millions of planets
following a Cinderella path and rounding stars
tiny marbles with blue water and green life

there consisting of the elements of star stuff
oxygen, hydrogen, nitrogen and phosphorus
evolved as bacteria and multiple cells
central nervous systems
brains with sensory organs
minds with images abstracted
through the Rebus Principle
to create symbols of intelligence

—just like us
but perhaps evolved with brains and minds
a million years before us to know
things only our visionaries dream:

the theory of everything
completeness of logic and mathematics
certainty of positive language
self-actualization of individuals
united justice of societies
unity of duality

—not like us
perhaps to know things
in our future to come
not even our visionaries can dream:

primal start and final end of the universe
another universe of unknown dimensions
eternity of time, infinity of space
death before life, life after death
the smile of God.

Like them out there
we are here
with infinite possibilities.

Birth of the Universe

Behold, the flash from far out there
energy streaming everywhere
Big Bang created with Sunday to spare when
God rested having bested all others:

> Archimedes was humbled
> no lever to move the world;
> Copernicus mumbled
> about God far away;
> Albert Einstein stumbled
> upon bent space and time;
> Stephen Hawking fumbled
> on information lost.

If you like spectacle spectacular
then buy a ticket and look for a seat
ushered by Father Lemaitre

> featuring the Singular Speck
> produced by That-I-Am aka
> Yahweh, Zeus, Allah, God

The curtain opens and on stage
the cosmic episode to be told
of a rampaging universe to unfold

dark energy as the fury of Shiva
hurling the forms out to entropy;
dark matter as the dung of Krishna
retrieving the forms back in syntropy;
entropy and syntropy falling apart
the ensemble frozen in the Big Freeze.

The curtain closes and the light goes dim
all are gone with nothing more to say
as nothingness reemerges as it started

The End.

Death of the Universe

If you were the universe
what would be your choice
of death among three bullets?

Destruction of Big Rip:
Bad choice. No one wants to be hanged, drawn, and quartered, then cremated into dust and
scattered into unknown dimensions, as you end not with a whimper but a bang.

Entropy of Big Freeze:
Worst choice. No one wants to die alone and cold, like Eliot's Hollow Men who fall to death's
twilight kingdom, as you end not with a fiery bang but a frozen whimper.

Reverse of Big Bang:
Best choice. Everyone enjoys expansion—more room from exploding stars and rogue planets
and asteroids, but not so for contraction as matter implodes back to its black hole mother. Still
you derive some solace from galaxies reuniting and returning home to relive the cycle of
cosmic life, like a family reunion recurring every 40 billion light years or so.

You have no other choices:
Nature issues no passes
not even for the universe.

113

Betelgeuse

on the right shoulder of Orion
with gigantic mass twenty times the sun
getting bigger and redder than all stars in the sky

this red super giant
with corona seams stretched to break
preparing the greatest supernova of the eon

ending ten million years
of growing pregnancy to be the mother
birthing stars and constellations for the future

occurring any time now
as the dazzling and ultimate fireworks show
lighting the galaxy to be seen across the universe

yet sadly dying as
nature goes about recreating the new
by incurring collateral destruction of the old

which also could be of us.

Hubble's Eye

Edwin Hubble saw far into space
    not stars but giant galaxies
    and cleared astrophysics of fallacies

    indeed two hundred billion galaxies
    moving across ninety billion light years

    and to his astonished eye
    speeding out in space ever faster.

He saw the fleeting universe
    not in a steady state
    like a well-tuned engine

    but a runaway train
    dashing down a dark track

    going out to nowhere
    no end of space or time.

Einstein shook his head
    and said, no it cannot be
    so added lambda to the
    cosmological constant

then saw the red light shift
    discovered green light speed
    out into the unknown.

Plato of centuries ago
    saw the universe destined to the
    eternal formlessness of khöra

    not something but nothing of form
    without the edge of space or end of time.

Hubble now confirms
    the wisdom of the ages that
    all things must end and go away

    as galaxies sail out to sea
    like Viking bodies set afire

    to disappear beyond the horizon
    of the unknown there of when and where.

Pioneer Ten

Pioneer Ten died January 23, 2003
its last message weak and garbled
then silent not to be heard again
gone in space 7.6 billion miles away.

Its whereabouts is now unknown
tracked last in route to the constellation of Taurus
the great white bull standing in the sky
representing Zeus once the greatest of gods
perhaps still there in the lives of believers
to receive Pioneer Ten and listen to its records
and Carl Sagan talk about billions and billions.

All living entities may end in void places
gods or movers or creators to be sure
also sentient beings and Heidegger's being
not of the dust of planets or stars
but of the cosmic or over soul
to be found beyond the constellations
and the space and time of human existence.

Then again, where may be the place of rest
for Pioneer Ten gone out of this world
like Eddington's infinite arrow
or for you and me at the end
of our short time of life?

Our destination is a destiny
not with presence in this world
but with absence out of this world
where nothing may be known
as accounted for by our cosmology
or dreamt of in our philosophy
or promised to in our eschatology.

We are destined to venture out into
dimensions before the beginning
of time and beyond edges of space
through the stars of Taurus that light
the way to endless possibilities
still explored by Pioneer Ten.

9

Science of Environment

Chain of Living

The chain of living is
eating what is below
eaten by what's above:

plants by ants and cows
ants by anteaters
and cows by humans

still the choice of most
steak or bar-b-que
eat rare or well done.

Behold the chain unbroken
of the eaters and eaten
always linked together, so

it is nice to be a human on top
except for the still unanswered question:
Is the chain linear or circular?

Once Upon an Epoch

Once upon an epoch there was the
beginning of the Holocene still when

animals and plants evolved and emerged
all in ecological harmony
thriving in a food chain of plenty
linking all species down from
sugar absorbing bacteria
and up to large cats feeding on meat

known as the Keystone Species for
the stone at the center of an arch
holding in place the structure of life
and allowing no domination from
predators on high to destroy
links in the chain down below

until the Anthropocene
when the hominid mammal
forged tools as weapons during
stone, bronze and iron ages
and summoned by a god to be
fruitful and multiply billions
to subdue the earth and
have dominion over all species

until none lived happily ever after
in a desolate tale where few lived at all.

Too Late

They will talk the talk and pollute the air:
maybe not, maybe so, maybe maybe.

Maybe it's not coming

    no time heeded because of
    political policies said:

    if it ain't broke, don't fix it
    government is the problem
    David Attenborough is senile
    it snowed yesterday
    fated by biblical prophecies.

Maybe it's coming

    still time conceded to meet
    biblical prophecies of

    beast of legend as in Revelations
    arising from the sea with seven heads
    apocalyptic horsemen riding over land
    released from the seals unsealed
    saved by seven angels with seven trumpets.

Maybe it's already here

present time needed for
natural catastrophes of

desertification and hurricanes
coastal flooding and forest fires
starvation and war
green grass turned brown
blue sky turned white.

Maybe it's too late for talking

just for walking

shovel in hand

to dig up land

and bury bodies.

California Dreaming

California dreaming on a nightmare day
a one in ninety-nine year drought of fire

and the grizzly bear burns on the red stripe
of the California Republic flag

and fires rage across Hollywood Hills
its letters exploding like fireworks

and vehicles are now equipped with
shovel, bucket and fire extinguisher

and green vineyards and orange groves
turn brown and burn in ashes gray

and Death Valley invades San Joaquin Valley
baking soil into sand at one hundred degrees

and salt water rises over beaches
as fresh water vanishes in thin air

and thirsty refugees go out east to search
but never to find the Colorado River

and Thales brings water in wine bottles
to start another California cult

yet on this unrelenting nightmare day
Mama Cass still would want to come and play

in a land of fantasy and fun smothered
by black clouds of fiery reality.

Good Times

Do you remember winter in January
years ago when we were children happy
to have enough warmth to make sticky snowballs and
to catch in our mouth water dripping from ice cycles,
good times for skating on sidewalk ice
sledding down hills too steep to stop
and most important snow days off from school?

Happy years then but happier years now as
I enjoy balmy days to stroll in the park
to drink beer at a bar-b-q outside
and not think about driving down to New Orleans,
instead happy to be living a soothing Midwest winter
free from the northerlies of snow and ice,
thanks to Exxon and global warming
and politicians who keep government small and taxes low
all bringing the good times of winters sunny and warm.

Do you remember those times and the winter of forty-nine
or was it fifty-nine? Tell me how it was, I forget.

Water Waves

Water ripples over
hard bumps of matter slowed
by waves of gravity,
always flowing downward
into earth to be at rest.

Water simmers under
waves of heat and vanishes
upward in soft air,
atoms disentangled
and entangled again.

Yet water's always here
within the core of life
in blood and flesh and bone,
its presence mysterious
felt by Thales long ago.

Water air fire earth
known by the ancient Greek
metaphysics of one,
as the four are still one
and the one is still four.

Stromatolite

You may have heard the daily news
about a rock green and odd that lived
more than three billion years ago and
thrived without peer for two billion years

also you may have heard unfounded news
about its death one billion years ago,
yet know its death was exaggerated
living today after five extinctions.

Yes, it still is I, the Stromatolite.
old and ugly, worn down and lying motionless
bound to the ground and immersed in a sea of salt
seeming lifeless, but no, not so.

I live as the first on earth, yet
you will hardly know who or what I am
but I shall be good health to you nevertheless
filter the oxygen and fiber your lungs.

I breathe in the sterile rays of the sun
and breathe out the oxygen of air
as an omnipresent ventilator
providing life support for other species.

I am the Stromatolite, giver of life
and creator like God, but more real
for still being right here, hard and solid
as the rock of all ages and epochs.

Winged Migration

From out of the blue
comes the haunting honking of geese
honk, honk, honking that all is well
echoing hope across the hills and valleys
riding the jet stream over mountains and oceans
high in v-formations cutting through clouds
up against wind, cold and storms
with strong wings on frail bodies

stalwart and endless
straight forward without dread
two thousand miles ahead.

From time beginning
their winged migration climbs the horizon
and begins seasons of spring and fall
as specks moving across radar screens
unerring without map or thought
knowing where to go with only instinct
blind over rows of farmland and sands of desert
high over skyscrapers of cities and smog of factories

irretrievable and destined
to return to the nest
where we all come to rest.

10

Other Science

Endless Science

Science journeys into endless frontiers
remembering Vannevar Bush's clarion call
to chalk upon blackboards squeaky and square
equations of everything here and there

> from the infinite of astrophysics to
> infinitesimal of quantum physics
>
> from Plato's ideas of certainty to
> Heisenberg's principle of uncertainty
>
> from Darwin's competition of the fittest
> to E.O. Wilson's cooperation of the ants
>
> from Skinner's conditioned behavior
> to Maslow's self actualization.

The scientific method travels all roads to
correct thoughts of common experience
debunk hoary myths of traditional insight
demystify beliefs not counted and mounted

yet forgetting Lao Tzu's call to loose knowledge
of measured judgments thought to be certain and
to attain the quiet harmony of Tao
that gives and takes all things in heaven and earth.

Circling the Square

Great square has no corners.
   —Tao Te Ching, 41

I'm moving down a line in space
irretrievably beyond time
not to be recalled or relived

    straight from a Euclidean square
    down a Pythagorean triangle

    like Eddington's asymmetric arrow
    one-way direction into endless void

    from the bright light of the big bang
    to dark silence of empty space.

I'm trying to jump off
this train going straight ahead
down the line to nowhere and

    to come and go and come again
    live and die and live again

    turn back to the spiritual flame
    of Nietzsche's eternal return

forego spirals to come
back to perfect circles

follow perfect forms and
endless re-creation.

I'm trusting science to find how
to bring around all things of
quantum and astrophysics

in harmony with gravity
of circles of spheres and atoms

when the center holds in accord
with Einstein's relativity

when particles obtain mass
in the field of Higgs' boson

where material bodies are circles
and all things come back in cycles.

I'm wanting art to curve the line for
the Vitruvian Man to endure

as squares turn to circles
and circles always close

making endings beginnings
and beginnings possible

and da Vinci never dies
to live in me forever.

Anthropic Principle

The feeling is always there from a
silent calling of unknown origin
translated, all's right with the world

expressed in holy texts as the word of god or
as constants of scientific equations
or in the beauty of a rose as a rose

known in the quotidian world of naming
as the Anthropic Principle because
we are of the world and the world of us

our human world born from star stuff
forged as the matter of nebulae
perfected as the blue dot of earth.

Yes, perfected, not just for earth
formed by gravity and placed in
a Cinderella path of grace

but for the magic of water and air
from which all life emerged and evolved
from universal laws of nature.

Our life emerged through the four eons of
pre-Cambrian life coalescing
from CHNOPS elements

evolved from the sea to the land
from fish to reptile to mammal
advancing through natural selection.

We then discovered words and numbers
technology using the four forces
disclosing still higher laws of nature

secured the constancy of truth
beauty of love and perfection
goodness of justice and morals

subscribed to the ethos and ethics of
cosmic compliance with human thought and
human compliance with universal law
transcended to cosmic consciousness

of primal causes and final effects
the principle everywhere the same

because we are of it and it is of us.

Misanthropic Principle

Not about it
all about us?

cosmic egg that fried
constant laws that applied
universe that arose
cosmic rock that froze
energy that spread and died,

planets and asteroids colliding
stars birthing and dying in cataclysmic silence
supernovae spreading across billions of light years
galaxies shattering the cosmological constant
and speeding into infinity,

billions of stars more numerous
than grains of sand on earth
trillions of planets—99.9∞ percent arid
matter 99. 9∞ percent entropic
energy 99. 9∞ percent nihilative,

atoms entangled and elements ejected
photons emitted from
fusion of hydrogen to helium
neutrinos emitted from
fission of atoms to particles,

A: A = A, A: A ≠ B
2+2 = 4
$A^2 + B^2 = C^2$
B = QA + R
$E = MC^2$,

logical/mathematical law
no human error or flaw
already there
earth water fire air
no purpose or care.

Not about us
all about it.

Light Thoughts

I sit by my window and see light
streaming down from the heavens
in an eight-minute journey
of ninety-two million miles

knowing science says light and heat
come from the fusion of atoms
of hydrogen and helium
in accordance with quantum laws

and trillions of flashing photons
spiked by indiscernible neutrinos
in a single nanosecond of light speed

described by the mathematics
of equations and laws constructed by
understanding of what is given.

Yet I wonder from where comes the
atoms and laws themselves
that bestow this show of light

Father Lemaître looking back
to see fireworks of the big bang
from which the universe sprang

the Hebrew God Yahweh claiming
credit of letting light be
yet he is a mystery.

Egyptians chanting Ra Ra Ra
to the god of sun or sun of god
yet either way light still seems odd.

All that said, what may be believed
science and religion must yield

to what Lao Tzu said about the
nameless origin of heaven and earth

and about nothing more to say
concerning where things come and go.

So I wonder how this light of life
came to pass and still now is to come

as light streams through my window
to make a path across the floor

and show the way to the ant crawling
past these thoughts that do not matter.

Oneness

Never mind the world:
where one breaks into two
then comes together with three
to fall apart as zero, occurring
in the moment of a thought
or cycle of the universe
said by logicians and laws of
identity, contradiction and excluded middle.

Despite the mind the world is one:
there and here, then and now
parts of a whole, points of a circle
end of beginning, beginning of end
black and white being gray
heaven and earth the same place.

As natural movement flows
human destiny goes:
Jesus chosen to live on earth
down from heaven in a cradle
and up to heaven from a cave.

And there never is a you and me:
only a we to be looked over
by our monkey cousin in the tree
who laughs at all our games of
distinctive numbers and names.

And there never is an i and it:
only an all recreated by
Brahma who sits on a lotus flower
and dissolves human-created lines
of edges of space and lapses of time

all the while with knowing smile as
we float through an ether of oneness.

11

Poets

Borges' Library

Of making many books there is no end.
   —Eccl 12:12

Borges and I
are colleagues.

We read books together
in the Library of Babel

a tower to heaven
extending brick by brick
        to God

holding books of wisdom
safe-kept and known only
        by God

We have a covenant:
my soul for the wisdom
        of God

from all books to read for
the theory of everything

      first beginnings
      last endings
      life and death

matter and energy
infinity and eternity

youth bargained for wisdom
this the reverse of Faust

this my triumph over the trivial
everything to be known, nothing unknown.

Borges opens the golden door
and I begin my journey through

levels upon levels of
hexagonal rooms holding

crimson hexagonal books
with knowledge of all ages:

etchings of cave walls

    hieroglyphics of early civilizations

      scripts hand-written by monks

        printings of Gutenberg presses

          literature from Shakespeare

            textbooks of teachers

              equations and mathematics

                news and historic records

                  digital documents.

My legs become weak, my body weary
my eyes blurred, my mind exhausted

yet always another room, another level
to dizzying heights, always higher

one more room, one more level
one more book to save my soul.

A Bee after Emily D

A bee straddles a clover
    sucking the nectar of life

        in the waning sun rays
        of a cold prairie fall.

This bee is dying on a clover
    clinging to the petals

        as the time of its life
        is now running out.

This dying does not matter
    only doing what it does

        without regard
        to revelry.

A bee straddles a clover
    sucking the nectar of life

        without sentiment
        its season spent.

Eliot and Fear

Celebrating our Prufrock love song
you and I go under a falling night sky
through certain half-deserted streets
by muttering retreats and old ladies
who come and go speaking of Michelangelo

but we end in a dark place where
street grime crackles beneath our feet
smelling antiseptic fragrances so sweet
hearing distant cries for care in putrid air.

We look to escape this place of insidious intent
now a space enclosed by labyrinthine walls
with windows of no light and doors of no escape
where nothing is heard but the cry of sirens passing by

and breathing in and out to gasp for air
and from the dark reaching to grasp my hand
you ask in a voice far away in space:
Are we safe?

Eliot and Hope

As the dusk of day fades to dark of night
and the journey ends at its promised rest

let us go then, you and I
when the evening spreads out against the ski

humming love songs with Prufrock on
cobbled streets with muttered retreats

passing hand-in-hand dimly lit rooms where
women go speaking of Michelangelo.

So we need not ask What is it?
simply go and make our visit

not as Gerontion grown old
and four quartets to God were told

not years counted as life's measured meaning
and lyric odes about its fated passage,

rather to make this new beginning
our walk together without ending.

Gray's Elegy

The poet tells how not just to live
but how to die in return to the
natural soil and succession of life:
Sophocles, John Donne, Milton, Whitman
and who better can say than Thomas Gray?

Better to die in accord with the prosody
of an eighteenth century graveyard poet:
no probates, wills or lawyers
no scripted services or licensed mortuaries
no news obits or farewells on Facebook or Twitter
no American way of death denied.

His simple burial begets a simple poem
in plain rhyme and iambic pentameter
painting a portrait of a country courtyard
as the day ends
          and a plowman leaves the field
a beetle takes his droning flight and
an owl mopes before the rising moon
all in enveloping shadows of quiet simplicity.

His vision shines on the idyllic countryside
then down to the graveyard, grave and death itself
as an expected occurrence of nature where
the deceased rests on the lap of earth,
bereft of anxious passions and endless wishes

in quiet dignity
        before the modernist indignity
of philosophies stating dasein never perishes
and equivocating existential self with infinity
and of technologies of AI-simulated monstrosity
of the dead living through algorithms on silicone.

Then there was no doubt, what death was all about
as commonplace as life, no cause to speak of strife
no drama of digital ending, only of spiritual bending
toward what was always there, not to mock or scare.

Jeffers' Prophecy

Goes the Age of Aquarius
    golden shores blessed with the beauty of Gaea
    and the purple wine and revelry of Dionysus.

Comes the Age of Anthropocene
    once the welcomed end of the Ice Age
    now the heat of the sun scorching the land.

Life on earth gasps for breath from the sixth extinction
    human unleashing chemical plunders
    burned leaves falling on dead grass.

So seen by Robinson Jeffers the anthropic poet
and prophet of portentous verse one century ago:

    Who basked in the glow of California of sun-lit ocean beaches
Yet rejected the comforts of human status and materialism
    A poet who rejected rhyme and meter and whose long heavy lines
Pound alternately on each other like ocean waves on rocks. A hermit
    Who sought the company of wolves as kind and ravens as lucky
Who invited nature to grind away granite and steel structures
    Of great cities and who cut by hand the stone of his home.

Who called nature the spoiler not sparing or caring, not faintly
    As nature begets us as her children then buries us back into earth.
Without God and wary of nature he stirs restlessly before death

As a cold and austere king sitting on a throne of not gold but iron and
With his sister as a treacherous blond harlot. He takes solace
    In being eaten to be part of a vulture as the sublime end of his body.

    Who told of the roan stallion won in a drunken poker game
Through the woman California who sought escape from torment
    Who rode him up the mountain and higher to the bosom of God
In a frantic rush to the freedom where she transcends to all
    And when the run stopped and the stallion killed her tormentor
She killed the stallion as a Nietzschean killing of God

Who spoke as Zarathustra the hermit who descends from the mountain
    Proclaiming the noontide oracle of deliverance from inhumanity
Foretelling the calamity of human subject imposed upon natural object
    Pleading his case to break through human dominion for inhuman
domicile:
Humanity is the mold to break away from, the crust to break through,
    The coal to break into fire, the atom to be split.

    Who praised soaring birds and stalking animals
Abiding by the laws of life survival without morality
    Perceiving the beauty of nature and ugliness of society
Embracing a universe of loving salvation and lethal savagery
    As a pacifist who would rather kill a man than a hawk
Denouncing the cults of Mother Church and Father State
    Hating tribal and national atrocities by lonely adults seeking a father
Who as the father of twin sons and widower of twelve years
    Becomes a forlorn survivor and forgotten poet of paradise denied.

So the age of gloom has begun in Aquarian California
where thousand year Sequoias die from drought
and the Pacific rise to reclaim life on arid land,
foreseen by a morose misanthrope or visionary prophet.

Sylvia's Ironies

Without a savior, Sylvia Plath as
self-fated Lady Lazarus can speak
only of the irony, not of dying
but of killing herself. This she calls art,
her calling, as if inspired
by a muse. She says
she did it right to make it real.

Sylvia
heroine of hell
mother of child
shamed bard of eerie irony.

Killing herself, Sylvia Plath
as the wife of Ted Hughes is
followed by the suicide of their son
then the suicide of Hughes' mistress
who killed her daughter as well
all from hell

Hughes then
writes a plea for clemency
and asks with innocence
"What happened that night?"

This Hughes
poet laureate of Britain for life
writer of children's books
burker of shameless irony.

Whitman's Song

The American dream came after the morning
of the Great Awakening and in the day
glistening of the vistas of sprawling seaports
and railroads laid across green plains and
through western heights of purple mountains
under skies open to an endless frontier

all envisioned through the poems of
Walt Whitman as an outpouring of self
not the transcendental self of Emerson
nor the pedestrian self of Wordsworth

but a self of the earth, leaves and grass
of good health to filter and fibre the blood
of common working men and nurturing women
of the American free soul and democratic spirit

a self of consciousness beholding life
beyond quotidian words or ideas
something still beyond real and ideal
from a thousand miles and nowhere found

moving in the wind from western frontiers
calling to come forth to faraway plains
fertile and inviting, feral and waiting:
I stop somewhere waiting for you.

He still sings his beckoning song
stopping somewhere on the long island
then known as Paumanok by native people

where grass still grew and leaves adorned
where the air was clear and water pure
where the virgin wonders of nature still stirred.

His song now fades on this Long Island
and unreal city of concrete waste land

its buildings scraping sky and blocking sun
lighting the night and dimming once bright stars
its sidewalks bustling with bodies fast-forward
hustling and busting out one door into another

its boulevards streaming with steel vehicles
emitting noxious fumes of roaring engines
its ports filled with ships spewing forth boxcars
of goods from global expropriation

its economy working people
not harvesting the grass of nurture

its culture fashioning people not
celebrating the leaves of nature.

But listen and you still may hear those
murmurings of Whitman in your ear
meant for all the people of your day
whose American dream went astray.

Whitman's Song Still Heard

His song of self is part of you
to filter and fibre your blood
into your heart and through your soul
shining out to the world beyond
at start of day and end of night,
and you know still in this time
across the land of endless space
he sits along the open road
in body turned to leaves of grass
always somewhere waiting for you.

Yeats' Musings

Young men leave homes to venture in
their vessels riding high waves and launched
with full sails to Byzantium where

dreams are sought of ancient gold and power
Greek Roman Christian Muslim cultures and
the perennial philosophies of sages

and stories since Homer of this loom of history
at the Golden Horn of clashing civilizations
and glory of Constantine and Justinian

attracting believers of ancient story
who journey to the mysteries of the East
and to the pleasures of Kipling conceit.

Old men now travel down Yeats Road
the worst diverging toward Bethlehem
as things fall apart and center cannot hold

seeking the revelation to come
for the best lacking all conviction
when youthful dreams are squandered and sold,

all that they grabbed having dissolved
seen disappeared and heard muted
by senses blunted from old age

lost souls walking down ancient roads
heading with hope across desert sands
but no road of Paul's epiphany

following a trail of uncertainty
traveled by the beast slouching to be born
where the revelation at hand was told.

Who are these old men but the youth
leaving home for cities of gold
in sands of constant changing form?

And turning in a widening gyre
above luring cities of pride
the falcon flies into darkness

beckoning old men to follow
and to still realize their dreams
on the road to Byzantium.